FROM THE RE]

FROM THE RED FORT

NEW AND SELECTED POEMS

by

FRANCIS BERRY

Redcliffe Poetry

Bristol

First published in 1984 by Redcliffe Poetry,
Redcliffe Press Ltd, 49 Park St, BRISTOL BS1 5NT

© Francis Berry

All rights reserved. No part of this publication may be
photocopied, recorded or otherwise reproduced, stored in a
retrieval system or transmitted in any form or by any means
without the prior permission of the copyright owner.

ISBN 0 905459 96 2

Printed and bound in Great Britain by A. Wheaton & Co. Ltd., Exeter.

To Eileen

Also by Francis Berry

poetry

Gospel of Fire
Snake in the Moon
The Iron Christ
Fall of a Tower
Murdock and Other Poems
The Galloping Centaur
Morant Bay and other Poems
Ghosts of Greenland

novel

I Tell of Greenland

criticism

Herbert Read
Poets' Grammar: person, time and mood in poetry
Poetry and the Physical Voice
The Shakespeare Inset
Thoughts on Poetic Time
John Masefield

edited

An Anthology of Medieval Poems
Essays and Studies 1969 (for the English Association)

ACKNOWLEDGEMENTS

'The Singing Dome' was commissioned by the BBC. Broadcast, the part of Jahan was played by Ronald Pickup, the part of Mumtaz by Mary Wimbush. The programme was produced by Christopher Holme. The text, slightly revised, here appears in print for the first time. So do, among the longer pieces, 'Mbona' and 'The Banana Plant'.

'Port Royal', 'Jamaica' and 'Closed Works' appeared in *Morant Bay and Other Poems* (Routledge and Kegan Paul, 1961), the latter being previously published in *The Times Literary Supplement* and subsequently in an anthology *Themes: Men at Work* ed. Rhodri Jones (Heinemann, 1972).

'Hvalsey' and 'Vadstena' were first published in *Ghosts of Greenland* (Routledge and Kegan Paul, 1966) and were later included in the anthology *British Poetry since 1945* ed. Edward Lucie-Smith (Penguin Books, 1970 and following editions). 'For a Ninetieth Birthday' and 'A Recognition' were also published in *Ghosts of Greenland*.

Two poems are from much earlier volumes. 'Murdock', composed in Malta during the war, after first appearing in *Life and Letters* vol 51 no 112, was published in *Murdock and Other Poems* (Andrew Dakers, 1947) and later in *The Galloping Centaur: poems* (1933-1951) (Methuen, 1952, second impression 1970). The sequence 'The Mediterranean Year' was similarly included in the 1947, 1952 and 1970 collections.

Of the poems here collected for the first time 'William Empson' appeared in *William Empson: the Man and his Work* ed. Roma Gill (Routledge and Kegan Paul, 1974); others appeared in *Critical Quarterly, The Listener, New Statesman, The Tablet, Poetry Review, Morning Telegraph (Sheffield), Angel Exhaust, Litsig*.

CONTENTS

INDIA
The Singing Dome   3

CANTONMENTS
View from Bombay Taj Mahal Hotel   19
On that same day   20
Incomplete   20
Parts Dispersed   21
Rescue   21
Warm Curves of a Canal   22
Muse Resentful   23
Beginner's Luck   24
Closed Works   25
International Bridge: El Paso-Juarez   27
Port Royal, Jamaica   28
Hvalsey   30
Vadstena   32
For a Nineteenth Birthday   33
A Recognition: G. Wilson Knight   34
A Touch of Asia   35
A God in Time   36
A Grecian Urn Polluted   38
In Highgate Cemetery   40
William Empson   42
Daughter Distressed   47
An Emirate   48
Carlos Water   51
Woodblocks   52

AFRICA
Mbona   55
The Banana Plant   66

FROM MURDOCK AND OTHER POEMS
Mediterranean Year   73
Murdock   84

India

The Singing Dome

(in memory of N.)

The Mughal Shah, Jahan, had the Taj Mahal constructed as a mausoleum for his wife, Mumtaz. Later, their son, Aurangzebe, deposed his father, imprisoning him in The Red Fort (from whence the Taj Mahal can be seen) where he was attended, for the remainder of his life, by his daughter, Jahannara. Dara, Jahan's favourite son, and designated heir to the throne, was executed by Aurangzebe, the head being sent to the imprisoned Jahan on the occasion of his birthday.

I

JAHAN: She is gone. The muezzin drones

Allahu akbar Allahu akbar
ashhadu alla ilaha illa 'llah . . .

'There is no god but god . . .'
But harsh his administration.
The desolation.
She is gone.

Ashhadu anna Muhammadan rasulu 'llah . . .

And that 'Muhammed is his prophet',
His 'rasul' — or his rascal
Rather.

For I will blaspheme.
Unlike his master, this 'rasul',
Required a woman.
Allah imposes this desolation.
He requires no bed,
Needs no woman to share it;
Requires no meals to be cooked;
Our male Allah never sucked.
And she is gone. For Allah
Imposes a desolation he's never known.

Hayya 'ala 'l salat,
Hayya 'ala 'l falah . . .

That drone:
Anguish of false hope against the sunset
For a king alone
In prison
As I, Jahan, am.

Red.
The red sun blares through the rising dust
Of the sunset, flares
Against the red walls of this Red Fort;
It stares through the smokes of the cow-dung's
Fires, around which squat a heathen
Cooking sour foods in each fall of desolation,
Or, fasting, shiver at each returning sun's rise
Of the disastrous curdle and Wheel of the Flesh;
Fleers through the flocked smoulder of its meridian,
Stunning the stoned roof of my desolation
In this Red Block that is my last prison;
Glares from its sobering smear of a violet;
Swooning to a grub-brown, in the hours past noon;
And, slurring,
Stares and purrs, as from a groove or stalker's slot —
Expandable with a hidden hand's tug —
Cut from a dun animal's hide.

And I have my one good son
Lost —
Dara, whose head was taken off
And sent to me in a blue enamelled box
Wrapped in a blazing gift tinsel
'With loving greetings and a loyal joke'
By Aurangzebe, the killer one
Of my loins
Who holds me in prison.

Unpacked, I meet my Dara's eyes
Wide and fixed, and my daughter's cries
Split the candle flames, and I forward
Tumble the table, knock out on its edge
My teeth at that rude birthday treat
Or banquet.
And Mumtaz is dead.

I watch from this mullion many dead heathen.
For down their holy river slide
Charred fingers, loosed scalps, burnt sides
And other bits from the blurred ghats
Which drift past bathing-steps or sodden rafts;
Then catch in the fishers' hooks
To be consumed or divided —
Idolatrous bits.

Nights.
      Dead.
            Bed.

Out of the nights of this my desolation,
Lying under the grained scarlet of this red prison's
Tightened sheets, I watch under the moon
Your mausoleum's dome
Lift, poise, advance, as if to astound
With your gleam.
The glazed dead moon on your white marble
Dazed. A cut-out. Too absolute,
In a geometry, is this substitute
For you in the swoon of the full moon
Since you should answer to each tone and each turn
Of that dead organ
With a dulled moan.

At your dome
I stare as the moon will stare, and long to share.
But broken the sleep, and slight your image, and the
    day
Butts, and the ignorant muezzin calls
His over-confidence; and the red sun
Stones my red walls.

Gone.

But why, in the name of the Enemy,
Sathán's, who wished us this harm, did you allow it?
You were at fault to leave me; allow him to take you:
Death.
Sathán wishing on everyone harm;
Sathán, making the wise ones flinch, and the holy
Cry out in their desert caves from his cavortings,
Shadow play, his fumes, his swingeing tail, his
    noises,
Obscene gestures — and you let him take you!
Saints, prostrate in their alabaster shrines,
Suffer his monkeying pinches. Hostile
To me, he is, and you allowed him to take you
    away,
Married, into death.

MUMTAZ: I had finished. I had been yours
For all those years; done all that I could . . .

JAHAN: 'I had finished . . .done all that I could . . .'
That voice is — from beyond death — your voice.
Or it's your dead voice in my live memory's ear
Only?
And you had *not* finished!
Done all that you could, but not all that I would.
Voices.
I hear your voice, and you are not here,
But I hear a strong beat, and I hear a strong tune:
'Re-surrection, re-surrection, his
Re-erection, his
Erection, his
— With a swing — resurrection of his
Erection'. The
Beat and tune
Of the Nazarene.

MUMTAZ: I had finished.

JAHAN: Had not; should not; though I hear
Your voice in my living ear . . . ,

The Devil. Sathán.
He made the stomach muscles of the prophet Jesus
Expand with expectation of food, only to contract
With the imposition of a condition
'Eat, but say "Thank you" ', with a wink, forcing
The Nazarene's bowels to a six weeks' denial.

MUMTAZ: I died because you wanted me to die.
Or thought you did . . . sometimes. For I could read
That silent thought in the way you looked
At me . . . sometimes. It made me sad — for you
Because I surmised you would be desolate
And helpless . . . I gone. And that you would regret
That thought you had allowed me to discern . . .
Sometimes . . . though you should have not.

But then, at last, I put you to the test
By dying indeed. For that I was prepared,
Knowing a bodily weakness — you did not —
Which I had concealed or, rather, hinted at.
And then — it happened. And then you thoroughly found out
The fact — what you had lost: your very best prize,
And your supreme friend. You knew yourself deceived
If ever you had thought me anything less
Or otherwise. And then you discovered
That you and I — through each year passed — had loved
The more and more each other. So you have grieved;
And I grieve for your grief, dear, that so I died.

And on this side I sorrow much to see you pitied,
Fallen, alone, imprisoned, old, and laughed at.
You have escaped — at any rate — to your comfort
The reflection of this state in a live wife's eyes.
My lord, I died to save your pride
Before a failure no man could avoid. And yet
You have the triumph of my monument,
And so I died to make that theme come right —
The Taj Mahal.
Your fame, and mine . . . It is a delight
Your pledging it mine or, better than mine, it's *ours*.
Thank you — I always thanked you — for it pleases *us*.

I served you with a complete devotion.
I was your secretary and your companion.
And your chaffeuse — for on the elephant
I directed that great hunk's direction
With an untrembling reliability.
And as for your emotion:
I, knowing how that land lay, commanded
Without your knowledge that I, being led, led.
I was your cook, your concubine, your entire
    hareem;
I managed quite expertly to your nightly dream
Knowing I was the really chosen. Now I
Would speak to you, intimately, although dead,
And flare you in the promptings of your mind
As far as I am able.
Wishing you well.

And although you are boxed up in that Red Fort
— For whether you ever get out is a matter of doubt
Even to me — know
I still serve you.
And recollect that I had said,
'Take another — when I am dead — for your
    comfort
But make then no comparisons aloud'.

JAHAN: Not your remembered voice in my mind
Only, but a fresh communication,
An advance in our relation.
Your voice is now and new, although
The vocal cords are shattered, and your tongue
Is eaten; your lips blackened; and your lungs
Blocked
With earth, and larynx choked.
Final gift. The Taj.
Your imperishable stone flesh, and roseate —
Out of my reach. And yet I gaze at
Your subtle skin as the day starts, shifting
Opalescent as the raucous muezzin lifts
Himself for another wind of his staircase;
Skin panting to white
In the shot of the noon or thud of the moonlight;
Skin that I cannot touch though my eyes reach
To your perishable parts
In the deepest dark below the dark floor,
Polarized below the crawne of the dome
Mausoleum
       or sign.

Sing, Dome, make that the sign
Your voice in my mind was not mine:
Your final gift not final.

II

JAHAN: Imperishable stone flesh, and your perishable
Flesh, known, loved, rotted; but to re-arise
— Thus says the revered Koran — or re-assembled
Into my arms on the last day — thus says
It NOT. I take it *so*. Meanwhile, in paradise
A simulacrum of your body lies
Cossetted — as you, Mumtaz, deserve it.
Cooling waters, delicious fruits, and pretty birds
Pipe.
       Not dark, too lonely; not glaring —
But comfortable half-light. We hope.
But no one can *know*.
Koran. The Christianity. The Jews.
Anything better than my heathen Hindus,
Providing the others die virtuous. For the pain
That the Prophet and the Christians promise
To those who do not qualify as sufficiently virtuous
Is a threat so horrible that I'd castrate
Myself and all my former subjects if I'd really
   believed it.
Hell for ever!
       Not even for Aurangzebe
Who has killed his brothers — as I once killed mine,
Would I wish that.
       For *him*, a just hundred years
Of his head being cut off, and stuck on him again —
Bleeding — to be cut off again and again, would I
   ordain.
Not everlasting pain. No, not even for him
— For Aurangzebe — hell. *That* is a notion
To make of good men, atheists. Better the
   extinction
Utter of atheists (Oh, no wonder they're so brave!)
For their kindness, of a hell, prohibits belief.
Better for good men or bad eternal oblivion
Than to be daily impaled and nightly flayed
For ever.
       Better the belief of the Hindus

With their gods and their godlings — better to die
And be born again as an ant, a buffalo, a woman
Destined for the *suttee*; better to be born
A caste gatherer of ordure, or a white
Worm, viced between the toes of a mud fisher;
Better to be born, and born, and born again and
    again —
After each stench and burning — into another
    condition
Than endure the official hell of our Islam or their
    Christian.
    Better the gods with six waving arms
Garnishing their temples;
Better their staring dolls with upturned corners of
    the mouth
Into which the green parakeet deposits his
    droppings
Without an alteration of their stare;
Better their bells and their marigolds, and their holy
    bulls;
Better their lying fakirs with their bushed hair,
Their tridents, mud-striped nakedness, nails in their
    fore-arms;
Better their gongs; better the washings of the
    heathen;
Their squatting in a circle, their hoisting up of *dhotis*;
Better their appalling doctrine of re-incarnation,
To become a blindfolded camel trudging its round
To the creaking bracket of a water-well; better to
    burn
To a life again as unhappy as mine
Than suffer the hell of Islam or Christian.

But if there is no hell, how can there be a heaven?
Re-union? and the consumation of all desires?
Beyond the dark curve of the dark river
Lies your body dark.
    Where is your ghost?
A prophet promises you that lovely park,
A couch, green silken robes, delicious fruits,

A ginger-tasting drink. Nothing about joys
Of intercourse with fresh winking boys!
Whereas when a righteous man follows —
I must qualify! — there will be those virgins, willing
 houris
With their spiritual bodies, yet sensuous —
But nothing of my re-union in the flesh with
 Mumtaz
Nothing of an embrace, until it blows —
Gabriel's Trumpet. And I suspect our Mullahs,
Who are fallible, often crazy, expositors
Soothe us with more than the text allows
Of that Koran. As for those friars,
Argued with by my ancestors,
What a queer man their Christ was!
Killed by those sharp trader Jews,
Fastened up on a wooden T-shaped piece,
With a curved peg, resembling a rhinocerous
Horn, under his crotch, for otherwise
He'd tear from his hands, and fall from the cross,
Then rising from his death and walking about.
A re-surrection?

Now, if the punishment had been *decapitatio*?
Would he have been seen around in two parts,
Together or separate? Sending into laughs or starts
His believers gathered together in a dark room?
His head a-hover above them? and glowing like a
 lamp?
Or if the punishment had been
Damnatio ad bestias, would the bits not eaten
Have bustled according to need? And those that had
 been
Chewed? the bloody gobbets spewed up again
Making the not too-damaged recognizable man —
Would they have been? Or *combustio*? Would the
 Nazarene
Have re-pasted and re-united his cinders again
In a way that my Hindu heathens' remains
Do not?

After their gongs, flying sparks, after the oven
A first and last soar of the atma into the Atman,
If they're so lucky. And no more burnings. For their heaven
Is no more body, feel, know, wince; ever unconscious
Of freedom from wakings, shivers, despairs and, O, our skies.

Incomplete is each prophet.

But Mumtaz died to make my theme come right.
And so lived.

III

This I had planned:
Opposing her mausoleum, mine.
All of black marble
Polished; and over the roll
Of the river, so as to join
A high-pitched tapered span
Cylindrical and flecked, or superfine
Serpentine; and glinting
In the glare of the dead moon or in the shine
Of the bored sun;
Accepting the music in its sad corners
The reflections of both on the long canals
Their casual
Echoes and descantings in darks and lights
Around the dome that is your tomb:

Your voices in my thoughts.

Epilogue

In all the Barnsleys, Bradfords, Oxfords, Swindons a "Taj Mahal
Restaurant: Specialist Eastern Dishes", and in Bombay
The Taj Mahal Hotel, Luxury and Tourist, but remote are they
The clerks at 'Reception', and remote are the restauranteurs *emigres*
From the vision,
Yet are concerned with an attraction:
Those two words *pay*.

But the Mughal loved his Mumtaz to such swish tunes
Architectural
That her death was swallowed, and rose into a delight
More niftily marble and swayingly firm than ever she lived,
Catching up the sun and astounding the daft moon
And winkling the gleams and the scents even out of that
Body.
      And the whitest One Breast of the East offers
Untrembling its double into the rigid canal
As you approach. Retreat, and appreciate both
The material and the immaterial hemispheres as
A simultaneous

Paradigm of the body
Of Mumtaz — not the moon's —
Dead as the moon,
     but yet elegant, alive
Half in stone, half in reflection.
        Neither College nor Town Hall,
In Oxford, the Barnsleys, or the Swindons,
Nor yet, of course, Bombay with its swagger hotel,
Has anything to equal
From the outside.

But a visitor may go inside

And down
To that tomb, under its replica, under the dome,
Where the crossed incense sticks burn
And may cry out
'Mumtaz'.
And that depth makes a sweet smell,
And most impressive, echoing around, is that call.
But She is not there
Or is marble.

So is Jahan.

Cantonments

View from the Bombay Taj Mahal Hotel

Pink fleshed and yellow long-haired,
Inept as a goddess at such tasks,
He busies himself in singlet and in shorts
As the temperature after sunset drops
In Bombay, in January,
And he shivers.

      His companion,
One-legged, but an expert in his condition,
Hops;
He snakes out with the ferrule of his crutch
Chips and shavings and burnable dung on the site
Which the barber occupies in the mornings,
And he musters a passable fire
And they warm hands, and especially the white,
Learning to squat.

Albino, no left behind in '47, a jumped-ship seaman?
Whichever he she is
It leans upon the brown man
For a comfortable brief blaze
Until the need is gone.

On That Same Day

He had watched her dying, had seen her dead.
It was in the early hours of that day.
That she was dead, he knew. He had accepted.
Certificate was issued. Registrar notified.

Now she is returning to her own front door —
It was the evening of that same day —
And with a sun blinding, a choking for joy
He cries out her name, stumbling to welcome her

Home. But it was not . . .Blinded
He was in the evening of that same day.
It was someone she had vaguely resembled
Once. With all that joy he had not seen straight.

Incomplete

With such a glorifying, such a heart-raising
Success. But that is what it was
And what is — is, and, thanks to you, certainly was.

'How disastrous it is to live in the past',
They are saying. Perhaps they are right.
But it is by your sweet ghost; it is from your sweet ghost

That I must breathe and carry on until that night
When it will not or — if it does — it should be right,
Or yet more disastrous.

Parts Dispersed

Beyond the middle of this our mortal life
I found me in a dark mush and quite alone,
Head in one place, bowels in another, and the gruff

Grate and coke of arthritis in the bone.
And the separated head it cannot understand
What makes the separated bowels belong

To a previous organization of a land
Manuring intellectually, or rather without will
Leaping in a joy where every part was bound

Up together: but in this mush no party shall
Quite have the sucking arrogance to say
'Money and possessions have the power to heal,

Postpone to die'.

Rescue

It hit the wire — and it — with a flash
Wildly, it — a creature — crashed to the ground
And there stayed, wings outspread; only a bird.

So telephoning the experts for a piece of advice
(Prudent, not a coward): 'Safe to pick it up?
An electric shock?' 'No, but it will be dead'.

But it was she who took up the thing in hands
Compassionately humorous, and displayed
The thing on a ridge aloft. The bird recovered —

That house-martin — it launched, drooped, and it rose
And it sportively darted, avoiding. It had learned
To thrive in its summer, a radar refined.

Warm Curves of a Long Canal

And the long long canals reply, reply
To that long loss which opens in the sky;
Reply that neither she nor Pope could get around —
That saving water in a swaying pound
Almost a circle; and the lock that rises, rises
Or plunging, plunging in a forest, flies
Stairs of interregna in a journey
From th' Age of Reason to the age of ferns
Threading the echoes of a melodious line
No woman has, but which feminine
A dream supplies towards a suffering taste
To sip until one gulps it as a ghost.

Muse Resentful

This Eng. Lit. biz makes me quite sick,
I'm tired with the factitious gymnastic
Of the 'levels' and the 'fusion' for the prac. crit.
Academic.

That 'detachment of irony' is a fuss
Turning my violence of luck into a nice
Precious 'ambivalence' of metaphysic-
al 'Wit' *(sic)*.

My 'images', my 'themes', are balls for a juggle,
My 'rhythm' a racket, my 'symbol' a bauble,
But this 'moral insight' is the most horrible
Cruel stick
Analytic

To punish my soft palms of emotion
In the name of a 'mature attitude', and now frozen
I'd rather endure 'the mechanics of plot construction'
Than the mean trick

Of Messrs Moral Involvement and Moral Evaluation
Who like to administer parsonical correction.
Lay off your acts of destruction, or I —
Who have suffered the economics of book production —
Why, even I
Might strike back.

Beginner's Luck

I once did a dowsing; holding the forked twig
Over a spot in a dim wood of Sweden.
And it worked! The two prongs in the clenched fists
Suddenly twitching, singing in the palms, and the wicked stem
Into which they ran, curling over, somersaulting and guzzling
In a hum over that one spot
Where there was water:
Focusing — sizzling — right on it.
Once. Not since:
I took the alder back, and it was dead dead dead.

I once did a flying; holding a waxed twine
At a point in a wind strand of North Wales.
And the kite lifted, it flew! and O the wild line
Reeled out and it whistled, and the yellow linen island
Sang out the rustle of its paper tail, but still gaining
It swanked and sometimes wheeled about in that plot of air
Particular, where
Parabolical delight
Said Yes. Not since:
I took the contraption back, but it was dead dead . . . dead.

ANSWER
Either (a)
Grateful for this and for that.
    And determine:
Grasp each stick of luck, and grab each swerving line;
Go for each down there, up there, or way out.
Or: (b)
    stay put.
        Dead.

Closed Works

There was a steep rail up from the clay-pit.
The truck, hauled up by a winch on a wire hawser,
Went through the doors at the top of a high tower,
Reaching there, was levelled, was seized by the two grinning men
(Grinning and waving to one looking up to them, admiring them)
Who, pressing a lever, tilted the truck so that the clay
Tumbled and rumbled down into the tower.
      Uprighted with a toss,
The empty truck, on a slack windlass, down clattered the slope
Jangling bang clattering. O lovely the speed, the clanging and
    ringing and
So to have driven one dancing or ruddy-faced wild with excitement
At the sight of the truck under the bridge where I stood, whether
(Whether smell of the nettles, the tar, white hawthorn in summer;
Or reek of bonfires; allotment smells, men on allotments in
    autumn);
Prying between the planks of the bridge at the booming and the
    slow and the upward long creep or
Glimpsing the jangling quick clattering
    a downward sweet swoop
Of the truck to the bottom: the bottom where it bumped and it
    rumped
On a beamy, wood-soddy dumbness of buffers, where it waited
For the tipping of clay-mud, the clay from, the hoppers
(Which men pedal like scooters round rims of the clay-pit
Rims round the clay-pit are railed; men loading the hoppers on rails

Then one foot on the plate, the other is scooting till, grabbing up
speed,
They lift both feet on the plate of the hoppers, so running till thump
At the funnel or chute) and how they would pour
The chugg-choggy lovely, the downy grey mass, into the chute
Dumping and thumping in the underneath truck, and then once
    again
The slow, the upward long creep, wire-hawser warblingly tight,
So grumpling under the bridge, and you peer through the planks
Of the bridge, and you see it — passing below you — the lovely,

The lovely, the loaded, the wire-pulled-up-through
Up-going, big-loaded, steady, thick-loaded
Truck
Up to the tower, where it levelled and stopped, was tipped
(By two waiting men, dirty their faces, but waving and grinning and fine)
Stumbling and mumbling its clay. Then righted
Clanging
      rang down truck
To the boof of buffers.
O, those Brick Works!

To-day I took my young son to show this vast excitement and
   glory.
But I find the brick-works to be now closed.
I attempt to translate a marvellously remembered text
But by necessity find failure.
There is an exhausted hole where the clay was used.
The rails around the rim are uprooted.
There are no hoppers; there is no truck;
(The bridge is insecure and the slope is rotting),
There are no two smiling men;
The tower is empty.
No noise.

Yet: All that was dug down for was built up with?
Or (more simply): Works Closed?

International Bridge: El Paso-Juarez

The Rio Grande's bed is dry at this season:
But a murky channel, under the middle span
Of International Bridge, still wets the frontier line.

Down in this channel wade the Mexicans, tawny
And raucous, they lift up on sinuous long poles
Lithe begging nets to those who northwards cross the Bridge.

And plead the nets, 'O passers to that rich U.S. soil,
Feed us your unspent *pesos*' — monstrous coins with holes
In the centre, cheap cupro-nickel, heavy, fanciful,
Figuring the Aztec sun god! And so cadge

The wagging poles, colliding boys, and so convulse
The tawny arms and swerving mouths for what is base,
A sheer heaviness to the returning tourist. Yet note,

From the advantage of the Bridge, one strapping young peon
Floundering in mud and in words, in singlet and damp shorts.
His working face is cretinous, his scrotum enormous.

So, sighting him, you toss
Your waste coin over the parapet
Though it misses (and of course)
The mouth of his stammer, his c-c-c-crying n-n-n-net.

Port Royal, Jamaica
" . . . wickedest city in the universe and the richest."

There is a melancholy in the bright sunlight.
"The Ghost of the Admirals who fought for us —"
They didn't — "is shamed by our neglect," scrawled, and
Elsewhere, "Literary *stop* And Debating Society." Lies,
Lies a man in the dust. The John Crows hover
Their jagged shadows about, and you discover
That in the brightest sunlight the blackest bile runs.

On the abandoned dockyard asphalt are
Planted pedestals, engraved, surmounted
Each by an anchor. Read, "H.M.S. *Aboukir*,
Blockship, 1902," "*Cataman*, 1886,' or that
— Vilely soiled — "H.M.S. *Wolverine.*" An anchor
Mortuary, and the edges of the asphalt lie
Lapsed in water since an earthquake. See
The crooked flubbed flukes of the anchors drain
Methodically a striation of shadows down,
Memorising a stylised rust in the white sunlight.

At the Gate of Fort Charles, now the Police H.Q., a
Magniloquent and coal-black Corporal flashes
The smile, and the scarlet-braided fine legs flash
An advance over the Parade Ground to conduct you
To the far-famed fortifications and the Curtain where
The illustrious, but then Lieutenant, Nelson fretted,
Scanning horizon for Villeneuve. The Corporal smokes
Magnificently, cap askew, lounging, and he lies
Improbable dates, impossible history, and he implies
Payment is due — American dollar — but the English shilling,
Offered, corrects his ideas. He denies. He salutes. For even
In this brightest sunlight lies a potential ruin.

At the end of the street of shanties there now lies
A new Club with Select Membership Fees
For best Browns and good Whites. The bathing-pool
Is filled from foul harbour. The fly-blown tables wait
Th' assembly of Kingston Importers and their ladies
After the sun has decayed, when the bar will be open,
When the money will be paid, when the dance-records be played
Starwards beyond the melancholy of a strong sunlight.

On the fast Palisadoes concreted road, haste
Past the Air Port to the mainland. All is shot
With an indirect discoidal heat, the air dins
From the throw, dins from an earthquake, dins
From hurricane 'Dora', dins
Ghost of Admirals, dins
Literature, dins
        Buccaneers, Debates, dins
Light on windscreen, dins

With lies, famous and infamous, Port Royal,
Hardly the richest or the wickedest ever at all.

There is a melancholy in the blackest sunlight
And a bile runs in the buccaneering town
Streaking the eyesight, and more insidious than
An English rain.

Hvalsey

I didn't want to go there, I didn't. I was driven
Denying I wanted to go there, creaking out Damn
To the demons with my boards, rasping out No-o-o
With my ropes, rearing, romping, rattling, driven
South of Iceland (there's the Jökull Glacier), driven
(The horizon is heaving), driven and driving
Kap Farvel around, and up the west coast.

And there I stayed
Four years, and what I saw
— Main things that occurred —
Will now be said.

First, and O last, there was the burning, but we'll leave that.

Now I had carried a woman, and do you know
But this woman with her rambles over three years on the
    shore
Got married to a Greenlander, and this Greenlander
(It was this, and not the other way round, I am sure)
Was a giant of a man; and they married,
Married in Hvalsey Church, and the church bell tonged
Till my very tall lone mast ached, and the bell tanged
Because of the bitingly pale blue of the sky when they came
    out,
As though every tooth and nail, and every nerve and tail, of
    my
        hulk
Dinned and stung in delight and washed in dismay.
But that was alright.

But what was not alright
Was the burning, and that was my third year
Here.
        I don't like it. Will not like it
Ever.
        Well, they said that this Kolgrim
— Greenlander, yes, but black-browed, mean smile, thick hair —
Practised the Black Arts to get her so
— Get her SO, you understand, the wife of the second
Carpenter (that's all he was, that's all he was
Tinkering me, the said ship).
Well, they got him
For doing the Black Arts, and they did him —
Greenlander though he was, and she only an
Icelander — in this way . . .

But I can't go on, I must go on,
I am driven.

They got him, this Kolgrim, and they judged him
Not of Adultery, but of Black Arts
Guilty, and they burnt . . .

This year, after the marriage spoken of,
Fourth year.

And they burnt. Wood scare in Greenland. And the bonfire
Attracted. And the sight. Attracted. And the screams
Attracted. Attracted, attracted, attracted, attracted more
More, more, more than the marriage
(And there were many, many were there a year or so
Earlier.)
        And the woman, wife of the second
Carpenter (she wasn't worth it, that you do know),
She went hopping at the burning, and, after hopping, mad,
Mad soon after.
        And leering.
                And dangerous.
But she died.

These things I saw
During four years compulsory stay
At Hvalsey (Whale's Island), driven, driven there
Without my knowing, or my will, or my consent,
Anything.
     And now they say
Sheep stray into the roofless church of Hvalsey
And dirty on its altar.

Vadstena

Yes, I remember the name,
Vadstena; on that afternoon
The steamer drew up beside the quay,
Below the castle. It was July.

I disembarked. And everywhere and everywhere
There were roses, roses, roses, here
Upon the castle and on the convent stone,
And roses in the gardens of the wooden

Houses. St. Bridget's *kloster*.
     And then the scream.
Rising and rising behind the bars
Of the convent, now the asylum, rose
That woman's scream, a sound of beating, soon

The roses shook in the sun as fists, and the sun
Shook like a colossal Mandarin rose, and there ran
Extraordinary grape shadows on the hot stone
Walls. Then stillness.
     Understand.

That was Vadstena: a scream, a beating, rising
As a gigantic reeling stalk and the roses' fume
Swelling all of a sudden, till their odour
Colours, sickens, sounds.

*For A Ninetieth Birthday**

Sir, what you give, we have and hold:

Magus, you kiss life into the dead stone;
The plain woman and the crazed man in the dull town
Make quick and green with loving; and make the moon
React to the stretcht dog's pain and the plant's groan.

J. C. Powys has felt the thuds of the sun
Startle the wild block of wood; he has shown
Us the Arthurian sword as down it shone
Yesterday afternoon; and he has seen

Unshudderingly the livid spear: caught the sheen
Of that hovering, oval, roseate Urn
Repolished till it throbs; has made the mean
Insect thrilling and ghostly, and the dead return.

Sir, what you give, we have and hold,
John Cowper Powys, ninety years old.

*These lines formed part of a tribute broadcast by the BBC Welsh Service on 9th October, 1962.

A Recognition

for G. Wilson Knight

For thirty years and more I have known one
Who has faithfully endured his vision,
Who has made an area of what was unknown
Possible, made much of the merely possible
Probable; one who has made us grow, challenging
Many in flesh and some out of it, who has
Prepounded the lineaments of a main adventure
For a generation.
      All this could not have been
But for a genius kind as great, honest as kind, which
— Given the original powers of that vision —
Has been consistent in its operation.

A Touch of Asia

An interesting relationship.
I do not know her name
But she is Chinese, and is
'Miss Wong' in my thoughts.

Pretty girl. Physio-therapist.
She is dressed in a white gown and a blue belt,
Pig-tailed; and she seizes my hand
(And I do not know her name)

And pulls my arm right back till it hurts.
'Ho, ho,' she cries, pain in my shoulder.
There! but to think one has to have arthritis
Before such another contact with Asia.

A God in Time
(Hermes)

Haunt.

I, in a heap of stones or just one stone,
Set by the roadside, haunt. I am waggish
I, without shame. O cunning. I don't atone
For footpads, or when snide murderers advance
To decorate the phallus which protrudes
Half-way up. Angle of One Two O degrees,
Sign of health, of genial expectation; I
Haunt these stones or this stone, rudely.
But O I am to be rumbled, rent, refined.

Not yet, though . . . Look, here's some fellow
Comes to butter up my organ. Drips in the sun.
Or another sidles up to ask a question;
Plugging his ears, and only when he's gone
Half-a-mile, unstopping them; and then the first word
Thrum into his head is my omen, a
God's, god's . . . O my haunted stone!
Over the years they groom it. O my hat
Wide-brimmed, put on my top, and on my feet
Sandals! Refine? On a gent they seem bent.

On a demi-semi-respectable one bent.
Dividing my lower half so I can run
Messages. Nude still, but IT declined
Decently, short, thin, flimp. Fixed once, I
Flick now messages on the sly
— A telephone — for masters, mistresses. Not die
It will, my organ, although my clients say
That *they* will die unless . . . *etcet*. What nonsense!
Hermes, experienced god, who has been stone,
He knows to have, and not have, and will not whine

Though now he is without. Once in every she
He'd like to plunge — almost. But I tell you this:
That now I haunt another stone. Praxiteles
Has made me marble — hard yet soft yet fine —
Leaning upon that heap of stones or just one stone.
And on my left arm sits the young Dionysius.
Far more than emergent gent, I am divine,
Quite marvellous; but am manifestly too good
For thumping waggery in a country mood.

But look what time has done to you
Praxiteles, the time. You cannot see my stone
Nor recognize. Your marble burst in the vein!
Cock broken off! my right arm at the elbow
Utterly lost! O, so I haunt, I haunt
But from a ruin and a mess, and I can't
— And now they're going to say I do — whine —
Be this, do that, until I'm made all one

Again. Museum restorers? Merely restored?
Critics, help such restorers for I can't!
For passively to be worked on is this stone.
But they do not know what that right arm held —
Those art critics, nor the dangle of the cock,
Nor its angle. Again to be divine! with crack
And shock of the Caduceus. For it's not
Just sighing for a groove, a vanished ground,
That I, guarding a god, myself a god,

Haunt.

*Hermes (**herm**, a stone) a patron of robbers and of libidinous nature. He had soothsaying talents. In course of time, from a roadside mark, he became a **courier**. The Olympian Hermes, with the infant Dionysius, is one of the few authenticated works of Praxiteles.*

A Grecian Urn Polluted

Pristias, the corslet-maker, has below
The walls of Thespiae a farm. Very fine
His figs, vines, lemons: divine Apollo
Being hugely flattered by a votive urn.

Hyacinth, on a verandah, blooms erect,
Safe in a metal jar whose panels glow
In the fires of the Sun as he arises
To gaze on his own begetting, and reflect

The initial scene, chased on the jar, and showing
How Zeus had impregnated the Titaness
Leto his mother. Enormous she was as
Clambering the rocks of Lycia (or 'territory
of wolves'), the wolves would leap; they sniffed
To nuzzle muzzles between her bare — O hectares
Of fine flesh — buttocks, when the Titaness stoops
To wash among the rocks. And Zeus sees:
Leaning from far above, admires the cleft.
      He plunged.
And all along her rich and deep kilometre ranged.

So on his own conception Apollo mused
And on his Hyacinth which the jar nursed;
Ponders on another panel, when at his noon
He dazzling polishes Himself new-born.

(Not storied on the jar, the spite —
Hera's green spittle-hate, which drives
Leto away from Lycia, and
Every other land forbids
To proffer ante-natal aid,
Bed for maternity, a ward
Or hospitality of any sort
To female Titan in distress.
Poor cumbrous Leto is from the juice
Of mandatory overbearing Zeus
Swollen beyond her first big size.

Not yet upon the jar was shown
Her pleas so piteous to Poseidon
To heave up friendship and to thrust
An extraordinary high tide up on Delos:
This god obliges, Leto flounders
To find herself upon a strand
That's neither sea nor yet dry land.

These episodes upon the urn
Or pot or jar not shown.)

See, Sun, Leto leans against Mount Cynthos' slope
(This hill on Delos is a hundred metres high)
And yet her head protrudes above its conic top.
And nine full years in labour leans.
      He drops.
Somersaulting, stands between her feet;
His golden head
Reaching to his mother's pubic fur, still wet.

But someone hated the jar, the god, or his flower;
And in the night that someone had pissed, had possibly gassed
Over and into the jar from which sweet Hyacinth grew;
Had spilled his mould on the ground, and somewhere obscure
Had done something ineffable — it cannot ever be guessed —
To the jar. Itself. Miasma.
      Pristias, the worshipper,
The anger of the great God fear-
ing, sickens; and, still sickening, of course
Dies.

In Highgate Cemetery

'Coleridge? Marx, Herbert Spencer, Radclyffe-Hall,
Down in the cemetery you'll find them all.'
With the *The Economist* under his arm, the intellectual
Sent us off on a wild-goose chase
Into the valley of tumultuous peace
And overgrown grass

Pursuing the tracks in a maze of tree-trunks and tombs;
Threading a jungle of flying angels, marble books, of harps and
    hearts, a jumble
Of creeds and of languages — there was a 'dear little Rosie',
And there were mysterious inscriptions; so treading a marvellous
Mass of ash and mountain-ash, of hummocks and ditches,
Of bramble, of bees, convulvulus, and everywhere
Messages of sorrow, affection, of pride,
Fresh, faint, or faded.

The keeper of the gates. lying on a bench in the sun,
Lazily volunteers his help upon our entering.
Yet taken at his word, he could not help:
'They're so many of them'. But he did presume;
While the gentleman, watering a new plot,
Did not assume: 'I only come as far as here'.
Widower, child, or parent — he was devout.

Treading the tracks in this maze for our S.T.C.,
Suddenly we came upon a hideous idol
Of him whose brooding presence we had forgotten:
King Karl Himself,
Dark with slogans, and over the cellophaned roses
Staring; and there were four live Bulgarians
Below, doing homage.
This wild place was no 'Democra-cee';
And they did not know of this 'Col-er-idge'.

The gate-keeper *had* presumed.
And what we should have said
Was not, 'How can we find?, but 'How can we avoid?'

Coleridge, of course, was in the Village church.

We're glad we did not miss that foolish summery search.

William Empson

I

An Earlier Poet's Hell
Often too sane, Cowper was at times mad
Outright. his 'Castaway'. On whose conscience should
Lie that? the Father's? the Son's? the Ghost's? Not ours!
Or the churches', inspired by love but teaching terrors?
'You'll be castaways for ever if you're not good.
Avoid:
Don't spell God backwards.'
      Dare it:
Dog.

Then hell. Despair.
On whose conscience lies this insanity?
His timid own? or that of christianity?

Nowadays we are inclined to blame the Reverend Something
Newton.
But was not all the mollycoddling he had of dear old Mrs Unwin
God?

Fear.
Like his own weak wild pet hare.

II

The Later Poet, to Whom Good Wishes, and His Intolerable Hell

When the object of homage is Empson, why recall an earlier
    William?
The later William's *Milton's God,* 'considered as a contribution
To the advancement of critical studies', may not indeed rate —
However consistent in its wit, characteristic in its hate —
Equal to the wiry speed of *Seven Types,* the splash of the *Pastoral*
(Brilliant on *Alice,* expert on the 'Elegy'), yet it is undeniable
(Not excepting the exercised precisions of the *Complex Words*) that,
In its No to the Christian hell, this *God* is the most compassionate
And the most compulsive Empson that this William has yet
    written.
May he write more, as indignantly brave, fantastically right

Or wrong — will live long characteristically brave and joyfully
    write
The books that he needs to, books glorious in a freedom from spite
But exquisitely naughty in wit. And may he rise — early or late —
To deliver no 'style of despair' but in his own cheerful spirit;
May he analyse the analysable, and of the indefinable
May he be less contemptuous than of the bad detective novel.
Then, cunning mathematician, *Times* crossword solver, may the
    surge or spate,
In his old age, of making verses, sparkle again, so that a *Complete
Poems* will double their present number, and may this contribution
By Empson be a crowning delight for this extraordinary William.

Fear.
But no timidity here.

III

The Sheffield Professor

(a)
In the teaching of a variety of text,
His policy was 'variety of opinion'.
Remember the mixture that he mixed:

Athiest, catholic, quaker, scrutineer;
Oxford, marxist, la-dee-la and fiddle-de-dee;
Post-christian roamer, the sweet-girl pagan.

Let us praise the jovial man,
His splitting jokes at various bars,
Quick chinese walk, the ruddy tan.

And let us praise the lucky man,
Chestnuts pulled for him from many fires,
Endearing helplessness, as endear it can.

And let us praise the plucky man,
His wit the stronger as the pain grew worse.
He'll end with pride as he began.

And let us praise the courtly man,
Concern for invalids, the touching airs
Of Wykehamist blent with Old Japan.

And let us praise the Yorkshire man
Emerging from his 'burrow' to stalk the moors;
In pork-pie hat, his county to scan —

Strong in the line of East Riding squires.

(b)
Witty and lucky and plucky this man.
He came as a legend, he left as a myth
At the bars, by our fires, with his verse, with his prose,
His extraordinary dares, his amazingly wise
Or — his occasionally wild, quite lunatick — flairs

He left with even more lustre than he began.

(c)
To finish this section — and with a grand slam:
Let us now praise the Sheffield burrow!
For eighteen sessions the Empson home.

Often from here, when disaster did loom,
Would he answer the Dean, or other such bother,
With an eye-weeping frolic, dispersing the gloom.

The joke a good way, confronting a horror.
A purgatory now, no hell hereafter.

IV

The Genial Sage

Hating cruelty, he hated hell,
All the christian implements of pain,
In gaols the rope, in schools the cane.
'More christian than a christian',
Say some. He'd deny it to the full,
Preferring Buddha,
     Loathing an idea of sacrifice.
     It was obscene.

At crossword, chess problem, textual crux,
Pet Algebra, wiser than Confuscius;
Choosy at cooking — Yorkshire or Chinese,
Detective novel for his evening ease;
At puzzling out this game of intellects
No-one shrewder.
    And then he rests, his face averse
    To mask of Benin.

Emeritus you'll be active. Marvell next?
Nervous as Cowper, you did re-act
More bravely from the start of Yokefleet story
To bestow at last on Sheffield your own glory.
And for all heretics, traitors, or others racked,
Did properly shudder;
    Naturally more generous
    Than Origen even.

V

What the Angels Said

'He jauntily attacked while others despaired
Of our Chief's unfortunate public image, and everyone
Forgave, except One.
    Look
What he said about Him in his *Milton*.'
And while they're busying the pages of that book,
Wing-fanning them over,
'We're lucky to have had him', conclude.
'For, about that unfortunate image of God,
This one *cared*.'

(1974)

Daughter Distressed

Earth opens, Sound of the rattle. Hades'
Urging of horses, 'Hi-yer, hi-yer.'

'O I have gone down,
And I can't see.
       The telephone.
Ring up. 0-6-0-Nine:
Mother? O wrong number, O
Get off the line
You impertinent young man!
O try again: 0-6-0-Ten:
Who's that? Marianne? No?
What? A Samaritan?
Try Thirteen Thirteen:
"A West Country Farmer"?
You bloody liar. I'll see you burn.
Hall Porter, Hell Porter,
Hail Porter! Hear your daughter,
Mother. O Mother, let me not slumber
For I am captured in a kingdom
And dial only the wrong number
In this near dark
Under tree root and a male mould
Smell'.

Sound of the rattle.
'Hi-yer, hi-yer'.

'Mother, get me clear of this man.
I am the Korë,
Yours.
    And I am crying,
"It isn't fair".

Find me, bring me to the surface.
Deliver me this year'.

An Emirate
(a man learning to drive)

Oil confronts the classic Arab scene, and
Outrageous overflow
By crude oil out of a Gulf land
Comes: passion from petroleum.

O-ho an outrage the
Coming in at my door;
Mad your immediate
Into my bed.
The merest preliminaries (no more) before.
Mad, perhaps bad.
Perhaps not. Not.

You in the classic scene, the
Muezzin crying out his 'allahu akbar . . .'
etcet , conjuring the romantic lack,
Ache or yearn — and O you were far;
The 'ashadu ella illaha illa 'llah . . .'
Leaks into the sunset, while the reek of the oil-
wells American's (scant B in that P) capital-
ism mix with last flares of that down ball
— *i.e.* the flaming sun — and your insouciant
Romantic yearn-ache ache-yearn then stretches
Away beyond the horizon's
Dust after-glow, it leans from your children
And husband, and away reaches to
Settles in me. O you cheat. O you nice dear
Among the rigs, the company dollars, and your air-conditioned
Super clasp-belted bungalow,
More than fairly positioned
In your fine Emirate.
'. . .anna Muhammadan rasulu 'llah . . .'
From you in a moderned Arab scene came a
Passion Lawrentian, and not a T. E. but a D. H.
And snatch into a flaccid Surrey
— The leaves of rhodedendrons aflimp in March —
Under me; so quickly; O match.

Confront. Affront.
Your *bedawi* in tents, not of black worsted
Camel hair 'leaking to the fiery rain' but of test-
ed nylon, darted with manufactured rents
To vent their fortunate inhabitants,
Nurtured on the power-producing consortium's
Thousand pounds gratuity to each man
Each year (none to the woman) and still each one
Endures his dry-throated black-tempered ramadan,
While his wives, muffled still against the Dieselled stain
Of the technicians' desire, crouch; and still the boys
Pubescent into the desert with their fathers ride
With their wild 'hoys, hoys' and their fathers' wild pride,
Swaying ceremonial knives, but sufficiently conscious
Of you, love, who watch them; and nearly half-admired
By a Defence Force consisting of our own Windsor Guards;
And wholly admired by you, whose interest stirred
Caught fire at my mast, and led to your assault
On a generally retired and careful sort
In a golf-coursed, a Betjemanesque Surrey.

Confront; affront. Contrast
The lithe nose-pinching bodies diving for pearls
And the quays for Japanese tankers taking on fuel,
Nips tossing their yen.
Not Charles Montagu Doughty's this but your scene.

Contrast the committed, or demoniac, drilling of drill
(Pennsylvanian all, nothing of Sheffield this steel)
With the derrick's abrupt shadow trellising the camels
In their back-side to back-side chortle copulation
Under an embroidered blanket modestly thrown
By the breeder, and the heat-stunned capped frown
Of the rig man with a sweat rag around his raw neck;
Contrast the Ruler in his Residence and his mile of tarmac
On which in flag-bonnetted car he sweeps to salute
To his execution square, where the rights hands amputat-
ed, stolen from robbers, gather, and all the gallons
On which you there, and everyone here, runs
From this Emirate
With me
Who am learning to drive.

Contrast; affront; contrast. Encounter,
O you sweet outrageous
Flush with the gush of oil, and the swell
Of American skills,
Expert in their penetration of shales
To produce a spurt so
Profitable, to seduce —
And in such a civil place —
With no fee, no royalty,
Such a civil me.

O you nice dear,
And such jealousy.

Carlos Water

Among the hazy blossoms of the May he rides
To the mere's edge. He sees. She has risen; or she rises.
Quietly she stands. The water to her hip bones reaching.
She is naked. Bosom with roseate points. Then her hair
In yellow twines over left shoulder hangs. Her smile
Intends 'You were awaiting this?' His eyesight mazed
In hers is helpless, yes. So 'Yes'. He was. She too.
    Then
Slowly, O slowly, she revolves, presents her back:
A hollow, black as charcoal, yawns, its lining studded
With crystals winking in the noon sun's gaze. Invites
Her dorsal chamber. Or compels. Dismounted, wades
He into the shallows of the mere — and will invade
That swarthy cavern of her back. It hinges close.
He is submersed.

Woodblocks

   Ghosts of Nippon:
Cite the 47 Ronin,
   7 harlots, 3
Inn chambers, cruel grippings
On 5 bridges. Acknowledge

   Nippon, you frighten
With display of numerals
   From your history,
Your 36, 100
And 51 aspects of moon

   Or mountains; 13
Foxes from waters; 25
   In Nagasaki
Burned, and 30 made headless:
Hitetada then shogun.

Figures to the eye,
Middleaged, of Hokusai
   Out of Kabuki:
But the 1, 4 or 5 zero
Thousand by the hour after

   In Hiroshima
Would seem to Yoshitoshi
   As blossoms falling
Beyond Miyajima's shrine,
The artist dreaming in death.

Africa

Mbona
(for Adrian Roscoe)

I

It is a matter of the rains or of drought
Which is the matter of our life or of death.
It is the rains: Will they be soon? or late?
Or none at all? Of when to sow? Too wet?
Too dry? Too dry the maize begins to sprout
Then withers; too wet the crop will sop and rot.
When come the rains? or, If they come? On that
Rests whether we eat or starve; we die or live.
Let right rains come down to us at the right time.
When to sow?
How
To make the earth mother and sky father rhyme
In rain flow?

Every year:
The rains? The rains? When will they fall?
Will they come early? Or, will they come late?
When must we plant? Will we be able to eat?
Or will the rains come not at all?

The village beseeches Kamundi,
"Kamundi fetch us that rain!"
Kamundi within the dark of his grass hut
Wraps up the foreskin of a dead king
Inside a special leaf;
He puts this parcel with two special stones
Into a green gourd and the gourd is then tied
To a strong fibre at end of a wand.
Kamundi puts on the mask of the dead king
Made from boa-bab tree, with coconut hair
For the king's head hair, and with a leopard skin
About his loins, he comes out of his hut.

Tall man, Kamundi, fierce, has white clay bands
Round chest and thighs. On top of head long feathers
Stuck in wet dung of pigeons spread in his hair.
Around the steps of his hut we gather and stare.
And Kamundi rattles his gourd that's tied to his wand,
And he stoops and picks up livid from the ground
Two snakes, they twine between finger of his left hand.
And Rainmaker Kamundi dances, shaking the ground
With the two snakes between his fingers also dancing;
He calls out — dancing — for the big drum's and the little drums'
    beat.
He calls out for our prayer-songs, and we our prayers sing.
And he demands of god Nmani that he forthright sound
Big claps of thunder in sign that Nmani has heard,
Demands, after the thunder, his sperm shower of rain
To make quick the belly of his big wife earth.
And Kamundi shout
"Naughty god Nmani, do as I say!"
So Kamundi demands, but Nmani is deaf, and the sun —
The sun burns up the sky — it has no cloud;
And the dust from the thuds of our dancing feet
Rises up and sticks to our bodies. Plenty sweat,
But no rains.
Kamundi does this three days, and after the third
We mock, "Kamundi no good! Kamundi
Rainmaker no more!" And then around the door
Of his hut we tease, "All the rain you bring down
Is our sweat! All the water you give out
Is your own piss water!" And we shout
"Kamundi, that old king's foreskin is worn out,
"Get a new one to stuff in your gourd:
"Kamundi, you've brought rain to us in past years
"But you're past your best. Hear then our jeers:
"You, old man, you can't do what you once did,
"The power has gone from you. Give up his ghost,
"And the dead king's foreskin, to another man,
"To Mbona, young Mbona, and let Mbona try
"Before, for lack of rain, we all die.
"Kamundi, we've planted the maize, and it's still dry,
"Kamundi, no Rainmaker this year, your magic is gone,"

This, after murmuring, we chant at his hut.
Kamundi very angry: "I the only man
Nmani the rain-god loves. I am the one.
Humble yourselves to me — otherwise you die soon."
Scared, humble, we say:

"Great lord Kamundi, sorry, but maybe other man
In our village do right things to bring us de rain
As you once were able to do."
"Other man!" yells Kamundi, "no other man can,
"And if other dam'fool man so much as try
"I put curse on him and he sure die.
"I weave special charm on him and he sicken.
"His right foot sure swell up with snake bite,
"His male member will be unable to look up straight.
"His woman beat him for that. His tongue will rot.
"I, the mighty one, will put spells on all you too,
"Unless you show Kamundi respect, pay him his due.
"And who's that dam' Mbona?
"Is he that idiot boy?
"That bastard lad? He have no father.
"That woman Mira brought him out with no shame;
"Mbona so stupid — to go to fool mission school.
"He no nothing can. He just write his own name.
"I make that Mbona die if he try to bring rain.
"That Mbona with one brown eye and one blue eye!
"That prove him wicked witch, and he shall die."

II

Drought, drought, day after day; day after day
No sign of rains. Kamundi go about, he say:

"Mbona grimaces to the moon, he wanders
"Among the bush spirits in the night;
"He's one eye proper dark the other blue,
"A sure sign," Kamundi claims, "of evil.
"Mira says she's never lain with man.
"How did she beget son Mbona then?" I tell:
"Mira swear she beget him in a kind of dream,

"A god came down to her, and with a stream
"Of godly sperm put in her, she started Mbona.
"Don't you believe in fool mission school stuff!
"When Mira tell that I have very good laugh
"Into her face, and tell what I think one truth:
"You slept with no good god but with a demon,
"The worst bad demon Mwana-Kanji, that one.
"Mwana-Kanji fuck you with his you-know-what.
"That's why Mbona has one eye blue, the other brown.
"That shows he's dangerous, and he tell lies
"If he say Kamundi can't make rain.
"Clouds come soon, I try again, and can.

"You should all hit Mbona with Mwassa grass,
"Tall grass with clubby root, got in de bush,
"Clout him with Mwassa club roots, and he die.
"Kamundi tell people more: Mbona, demon's son,
"And slut Mira's. He cast evil spells. I warn
"He make pregnant woman give birth to cripple —
"That white man's blue eye does it. When a man
"Goes off into de bush and not return
"The reason is he's been turned into a stone
"By Mbona. He turn himself to scorpion
"And sting nice woman he can't lie upon.
"He bring rain! No, I bring rain, and then
"He bring de locust eat up all de maize grown,
"Same as last season, when the big gold sun
"Went black as night, and with *whirr-whirr* the swarm
"Came over the horizon. and on and on —
"You weeping and screaming — on our crop settle down
"And tear tear with devil teeth, and when locusts gone
"Just stiff naked stalks left. You starve!
"That Mbona's doing. Mbona very jealous
"Of Kamundi. People, remember Mwassa grass,
"Its clubby roots. And Kumandi try again
"To-morrow noon to bring down much needed rain."

We gather and dance and Kamundi once more
Tries, but of rains not a drop, and de skies burn,
But one cloud shows, and that is cotton-tree white.

Kamundi stamp angry, swears he'll get another foreskin
To put into his sacred gourd, and two other stones,
And another mask of yet older dead king.
But we murmur,
"Kamundi is afraid
Of Mbona. Why is that
He hate him so? Maybe the dead
Know better, and this Mbona is touched
Or reached
By ancestors to save our lives".

Mira dotes upon her simple child,
"Mbona, my sweet, my only son,
"Precious Mbona, my pretty one."

Simple! He could neither hunt, nor trap, nor fish,
Could scarcely handle digging stick or hoe,
Yet Mira thought him special, he'd eye so blue —
A sign to her that he had magic power
Though he had never put it yet to use.
Mira and Mbona were scorned by every neighbour.
Mbona, sixteen years old, declared at times
Strange people came to visit him in dreams.
At day break, with head upraised, he'd wildly talk
To unseen persons, or his legs and arms would work
Whirling, and he'd fall down in sudden fits.
They say he'd leave his sleeping plank at night
To go bush rambling to the dreadful ju-ju pole.
And on this pole was fastened with a nail
A rotting scalp and a large left hand, a male
Witch's, convicted by the tribal court
Of going around the village as a spotted cat,
Causing much sickness. He was brought to trial.
Chief witness was Kamundi. At the ordeal
This man was bidden eat five bits of glass;
If he were innocent these he could pass.
He couldn't. The Mamba snake was put to him. "He die,
That prove his guilt for sure", Kamundi say.
At the foot of the ju-ju pole a chicken beak,
A white man eyeball in a little box,
Some bones, the white man's beard beneath a stone.

"Why Mbona go ramble to the ju-ju pole?"
We ask. "All de same, why Kamundi scared
Of Mbona that he curse him? Maybe
Mbona makes rains come. We go to house
Of Mira, tell Mira if she will please
Argue Mbona to come out and save us
By making rain." We go round in a crowd,
Headman among us, to Mira's and Mbona's hut.
Mira out to meet us. Mbona deep in the dark
Crouching slyly away right in the back
A-cuddling a cat, see its green eyes stab-stab.
We hand her — squark-flutter — live chicken to eat.
We say we think she's right "Your Mbona is better
At making the rains than old Kamundi. Pray Mother,
Argue your good son out, persuade him try
To make the rains to-morrow, or we'll all die."

"Dearest Mbona, sweetest boy,
"Save your people, bring them joy".

Mbona comes out, is proud, says he will try
On the morrow. We bow. We thank. We go away.

III

We all gather round Kamundi's big hut.
Kamundi stalks out on steps of it to watch.
We make dance circles — women inner ring, men outer ring.
Mbona is put in middle of rings. He wear no mask,
Has no calabash or gourd rattle, no charm things. He just stand.
But he lift up his brown eye and his blue eye to sky,
And he lift his right arm straight up to the sky,
And we

Dance, how we
Dance, and de king drum how he
Beat
Skin of goat, din of goat
Drum-a-drum, and we, how we
Jig-a-jog jog.
Clank soon our necklets, bang our bracelets, clang our anklets,
Bounce then our bubbies, our gee-gaws zing-ring-zing, and our sweat pours
Shaky and shiny, as we women jump-thump, and we men thump-jump,
We women jump thigh high; we men's spear hafties dump thump in the mound ground.
Our lips foam frothy, our white clay melty,
Our king drum tom-toos tom-toos thumping, our blood life pumping
Sumping
Louder, prouder, our white-of-eyes wider wilder
Baring staring glaring
As king drum tom-toos tom-toos,
Tom-toos, toos-toos
King drum drum king
Tom tom tom toom tom
And in our prayer-dance sing we, ring we, vow we
Thank yous to rain-god Aranje, to thou we —
If he send down rains, if he put stop to hunger pains.
That we-all-together-men cry, "Mbona make rains! god bring down rains!"
Then we all-together-women cry, "Mbona make rains! god bring down rains,
End pains!"
And we men and women in big prayer call then:
"Mbona, bwanal, Mbona, rains make.
Give us dat luck,
Make sky rain cloud de dry earth fuck.
Kamundi try but no longer strong, Kamundi too weak,
Though Mbona be young, he is yet strong, Mbona rains make."
Our prayer song begin to work
We sing

"I see cloud, we see cloud,
Big cloud, loud-with-thunder-cloud,
Come now, proud-with-rains cloud, this way
Come, go on growing now
Over Mulanje.

Cloud, look at Mbona, there he stand.
He wear no mask, he wear no clay,
He rattle no gourd rattle, he stand quiet
In de middle-of-de-dance rings.
He no dance or prayer sing.
He be quiet on his feet, quite.
See, Kamundi watch him. Mbona's no fear,
Mbona's no special gear,
No dead king's foreskin in rattle gourd, no leopard skin,
But he stand bare, he has no fear,
He young, he thin,
He stand quiet".
But
Sudden he lift up his right arm straight
Up high,
Direct up to sky,
And his left arm shoot up bent at de elbow,
So left wrist is on elbow of right arm so.
And his two eyes, one eye dark, de other blue
Look up straight to you
Aranje, god Aranje
Come from Mulanje
In big cloud, rains cloud,
Rains-with-thunder cloud.

And then it come
As de king drum drum
FLASH

Such a FLASH as no man ever seen
In all years gone
Or ever been.
Lightnin'!
Zigg-a-zigg-zagg

Dat golden fire
Run like quick snake make along de ground
Just where Mbona stand
(It frighten Kamundi, we bet,
Even if he angry mad),
And we all cry out, "Ware, ware,
Look out, fire!
Count out three! Three!"
One, two, three, and big thunder boom
CRASH
So loud the fear of it made woman's shit come
And scare even de brave man:
Such a crash as no woman had ever heard,
It make even de brave man afraid.
And de rains pour down, roar down.
Lift up our faces, our faces get bloody wet,
Faces wet, women bottoms shat,
We don't mind that,
We drink water through white teeth and laugh at it,
Rain sop hair, rain down back kisses,
It hisses down, it pisses down,
It run down bottom, it run down breast,
It make dank and clammy all de rest,
Ding-a-ding dong, ding-a-dong dong
Dis our song:
"Rain is coming down
And we don't care so long as we don't drown,
As long as maize blades shoot, come up soon,
Come up lovely green,
Make us good food
From ground we have hoed.
Rainmaker Mbona has been
He give us life."

Rains are falling; maize is sprouting;
Dance we happy; laugh our children;
Praise to Mbona; sing we cheerful;
Smile in rainfall; hands are clapping;
Leave our meeting; skipping joyful;
Run to maize fields —

      Quick. Quick. Stop!

IV

For not before
Kamundi curse
From de steps of his big house:
"Dat Mbona very-bad-man-witch,
He do dese
Rains through me, he couldn't do no such
On his wicked own. He couldn't do no much.
Through *me* has Mbona done.
I, Kamundi, pass
Sentence. Pull up Mwassa grass,
Beat him with it till he die.
Strike him in his evil eye.
Mbona be worst of dam' witchcraft boys.
If justice be done, he die."

Days pass,
Boys go into bush, dig up Mwassa grass,
— Mwassa tall plant, stiff plant, its root
A hard white ball. Den dese boys,
With much Mwassa, go around Mira's hut,
And dey cry, "Mbona, Mbona, come out, come out!"
And when he come out dey give him de chase:
"After him! After him!", like in a big race.
But dey catch him, and swing the ball roots in his face,
Dey hit him in his blue eye, and he run
Holding his hand to his face. Den we women and men,
Hearing the noise, follow, share in the fun,
Cry, "Stop it you boys; give us that Mwassa grass".
We take de Mwassa grass from de boys
And we drive Mbona with blows to before Kamundi's house,
Buffeting him on back, belly, bottom. face
— Long plant, hard root — hit him all over de place.
Till blinded, Mbona he fall, and sobbing he cries,
"I brought you de rains, you kill me for dat." "He shall die,"
Kamundi shouts, "Dat's proof of his sorcery.
Take off his head and hands, and on de ju-ju pole

Fix them below the scalp. Mira, and you all,
Know her bastard blue-eyed son be wicked witch.
Trust in Kamundi. And, if you want to thrive,
He bring you rains next year. In me have faith,
Kamundi Rainmaker. Know I am such."

Mbona's head and hands on ju-ju pole
Are fitted. Other Mbona parts, men say,
Taken up path to flat-top Zomba hill
And thrown down deep hole. Men call it Chingwe's hole.
And that is Mbona's tale:
'Myth of Chingwe's hole," white men say of it.

Mira went crazy ill, die soon. Kamundi live still.

He . . . powerful.

The Banana Plant

He had two wives. Magépo was the senior;
Mkundikana was the junior; and each
The rival of the other. But their husband
Magépo's house or Mkundikana's house
Visited as his desires inclined.
Magépo, Mkundikana — each had skills
Was hers and hers alone. Magépo made pots
Shaped by devoted hands. Lovely they were,
White, round, shiny as a cowrie shell.
Mkundikana's fingers fashioned baskets
Subtle, more intricate than a spider's web.
And with examples of these arts, they vied;
Strove against each other for his favour.
Vexed by their squabbles, their man at last declared:
"Tomorrow Magépo bring here your finest pot;
And Mkundikana bring here your finest basket;
I'll judge which of the two shall have the prize,
The winner of the prize shall be my favourite."

Next day the women came. Magépo kneels,
In her small hands she holds up high her pot;
Big Mkundikana does not kneel, but stands,
Clasping her basket to her bosom, smiling.

The man looks down upon the pot. Delicate,
Yet firmly gleaming in the sunshine — this:
A perfected shape of her adoring hands;
And she — Magépo — offering it, now pleads,
"This is the best that I can do. Accept.
I've tried to please you always." Slender, white,
Curved like a polished cowrie shell, it shines;
Faultless but frail like her, Magépo's self.
Mkundikana advances then a stride,

Extends the basket from her bosom, "Look,
And in the cunning of a craft admit
No-one excels, or equals me. I cut
Sorely my fingers intertwining twigs,
Sharp from the bush." Seeing Magépo's pot,
Mkundikana's basket, the husband is
Caught in their gleam or maze of beauty, but
He must decide.
      He says, "Give both to me.
Mere sight alone is not enough to judge,
My feel for soundness is a further test.
In his right hand he takes Magépo's pot
About its neck, and in his left the basket
By its carrying loop. He weighs them both.
Weightier is the pot. "But not so strong",
Claims Mkundikana, test them for that.
Cast both upon the ground about our feet,
See which is sturdier when misfortune falls."
He raised his arms, "Go on, you dare not throw!"
"Don't risk too much," Magépo pleads, "You'll throw
Me from you, love." Trusting too much, he throws.
The basket dances on the ground unhurt;
Smashed in pieces is the glowing pot,
Scattered its fragments. "You have broken me,
Your Magépo. Was that your real wish?"
But bouncing, sportive was the basket, quite
Game, undamaged. Mkundikana pleased,
Flashes her teeth in smiles. She stretches, tall.
Magépo still is kneeling. Surprised, in tears.
So Mkundikana succeeds as favourite wife.

Soon after this Magépo's blown away.
"I shall be near to you in heart", she says;
"You'll not forget." Nevertheless she's blown
Away, she passes, She's buried under the earth
Of the unroofed walled compound of her own house.
The husband sleeps in the house of Mkundikana.

The months go by. And Mkundikana smiles
Less often over the cooking stove, in bed,
And takes less pleasure in her basketware.

She notices her husband leaves her house
Often, daily, and on his shoulder bearing
A pitcher heavily laden. Mkundikana
Watched his goings, waited for his returns.
To her enquiries would he answer nothing.
Yet was that pitcher of Magépo's making?

One afternoon, her husband having returned
With the pitcher empty — and now he's sleeping —
Mkundikana's able to restrain herself
No longer.
    Straight to Magépo's house, she goes;
Enters the door of Magépo's walled compound,
And sees what she'd expected. There it is:
Sprung from her grave in the small compound's centre
The young banana plant. Freshly watered,
Healthy, vigorous; gracefully its leaves
Fanned the beaten ground in cooling shadows,
From underground the stem, or false trunk, grown
Out of hidden clump or stool. See how it hangs
Its soft yellowish flowers. Moist the soil,
Mellow the air, gorgeous the promised fruit,
The occasional breeze, not brisk enough to tatter
Or shred, but setting astir the broad leaves
To wave and wander delicious arcs and whispers.
Laminate that glossy green stem, each joint
Cupping and cusping the one above, a song
Of a youthful confidence supreme — its sign:
The goldenish rosette at the summit, from which it thrusts
Eight yellowish spikes, from which would come
The prodigious ripened hands — Magépo's fruit.
So Mkundikana knew.
Daily he'd come to water the bed of this plant
With a pitcher brimmed with his tears. So dear!
She interred? Under that bed, her life
Feeding that false trunk!
    Ablaze with anger
Mkundikana left Magépo's for her own house,
And for a bushknife.
    Returns with quick long steps —

Door swinging on its hinges — and with one slash,
At knee height from the ground, she severed the stem,
The upper part toppling with a hurrying sigh of its leaves.
And, from the hole in the neck of the stump, there gulps
Out blood nearly black, and from that tube there spoke,
Between the gulps, the words of Magépo:
"At last I'm truly finished, but my end
Will be yours too Mkundikana".
    The stump withers,
Would not renew with tears, but still the husband
Remembers it green, and even Magépo alive
And loving, for then how surely he had been
The most favoured of men.

From Murdock And Other Poems

Mediterrean Year

I

A Salvo for Spring

Licking, the fires of the Spring are now rampant,
Memories jostle with lusts,
Flaring as tulips their bursts;
But jesting and silken our Marshal flamboyant
Topples regret in the lists:

Over the hills the Horn is now heard, —
Reveillé revealing the runaway seed.

Man 'o the air is now chromium precise
Engages the sky with a plane;
The Huntsman approaches with Horn;
And flecking and flitting through flexible trees
Purrs the jaguar sun.

Snarling and whisking it slaps out its banter,
Drums from arcade the herd in a canter.

Golden in gongs is the Spring in its thunder,
Crashing the marriage of whales in a flounder,
And seas run amber in bands,
Zebra is sireing on mounds,
Giraffe is stallion on Rands,
Cocoons are snapping their bonds,
Cobras are tangled on sands,
Bucks are rutting in bounds,
And tiger and hands seek pillage and plunder
And Love is a furnace of wounds;
Blood-striped the bliss, and anguish the wonder

As ardour's rash fumble, the red of desire
Rises to sing cantata of fire.

Tiger lily, tiger moth and tiger
Sidle and rinse in their bars,
Slink in the shine of their furs;
Leopard and foxglove in stars
Wink and then wheedle; to Huntsman's gay trigger
Lollop and snuffle the boars
And carnage bespatters the flowers:

Iris and tusks sing game to the gun
Gleaming to gain a quick unison.

Gone not the past and the future not come:
Tears for a friend in his death
Sepulchred far on a heath;
Eye for companion in stealth
In copses to garner her tilth;
So prayer and a praise in a flame and a fume
Marry together in hum
Murmurs an ordorous bloom:

Sun and the sprays on causeways are twined,
In prison of rays they prism the wind.

March with its winds and its sun goes shares,
The mind is haunted and hastened with flares
Red as the stallions' rears
His eyes asunder like scars
Yelling Asiatic for slaying in wars
Neighing for support from mares;

And Tambourine resounding from the cave
Clangs its cadenzas on the echoing grave.

Huntsman in damask steps out of the glade
Raising his Horn to his mouth.
Bloodstained, he's hairy, he's Truth;
So bury the limping, the sick and the mad,
Embracing hurrahing his Life:
Crimson her blushes the dark-favoured Queen,
Happily hears the tart tambourine.

Advances our Huntsman, his woman he brands,
Irons out stipples and creases,
Springtide her womb now so fresh is;
Sun thumps down on the seas and the strands
Regarding and shining on ecstasies:

And submarine and cold in capers and gold
Fishes now flirt in their dances emerald.

And submarine and cold in capers and gold
Fishes now flirt in their dances emerald.

Hunter, O Sunburnt, O braggart does now
Harries harrahing her rose,
Getting those brave ones, these boys, —
For Autumn will come and with its smirk and its bow
Ending in mist and in moss.

Bathing are boys the delicate strong
White in the clang of tambour's bright gong.

September will come in its tatters and tunes,
Regret will tumble in rain
Speckled and mingled again;
Death will go crying with its duns from its dunes —
"Both Huntsman and Horn are in Vain":

Then deep in the woods the Horn is laid down
And low in the vaults the tambour makes moan.

II

Centaurs at Solstice

The Sun, beribboned Archer, rides
Twanging his Arrows on hides
Of Centaurs, who rear and run with the smart,
Shake fists (their Man-flanks heave and Animal sides);
They shout to shade and shunt on barks in their hurt,
Sighing for drink, with bloodshot eyes they paw in the glade,
Scratch sores, drip foam, and whisk their tails at the gad.

Tear-stained and raw the Centaurs brood,
Bough-hidden lust for Thracian maidenhood,
The long-limbed girls with gold hair bound in snood.

The Sun, a Soldier-Sovereign, hurls
Brass balls through tubular halls
Of light on Cyclades and Crete:
Lands stutter in chequers, grimace then settle in whorls;
The sulphurous plains start humping or flatten in heat;
Stromboli itches with spray or crapular crawl of its soot;
Goat, tethered to stump, nibbles and coughs at the root;

Then bleared and sad the Centaurs plod,
Noon-bored fidget, trample hooves and prod
At balls of mud — or, sudden, stamp insects dead.

Noon Sun, an Artisan at forge,
Dins his hammer on targe,
And Lipari Isles twirl whinnies of smoke;
Land-slabs with cactus beards split wide with rage;
The puff-toad stares and yawns midway his croak;
Felucca's sail is slopped; the Libyan deserts crook
Their voilet snibbing mirage in cavorting mock.

The Centaurs bestrides the carob log,
Massage their bellies, day-dream of piston dark
And of its quadrupedal two-arm work.

The Sun, a tasselled Trumpeter, brays
Shivers of silver rays
On knife that flicks castrating wound;
On Enna where the jerkined lizard sways
And casts his tail with yellow smear to ground;
And blares on Thessaly, where the white boy in the sun
Disdained his apple Venus when she'd his clothes undone.

Centaurs wrestle in pairs, guffaw,
Or, playing tag, smack fleeing after-quarters
Which buck and swivel, or comb their hirsute torsos.

The Sun, a zooming plated Cup,
Swills round its coppery syrup,
Spills it on cactus till its's stiff
As Greek flogs his panniered donkey up the slope;
Piazza lazars grub for pavement stuff;
As females, straddling thighs, let water into Nile,
The Cypriot felon's shot with moustachioed smile.

In glades the Centaurs plot their raid —
How with a whoop the Leader'll wheel, and loud
They'll catch the maids and thud return to wood.

The Sun, a fat white Disc of Bone,
Squirts its marrow at noon
On horses dead, distract, whose swollen bellies
Winkle and hum with sucking flies — till Moon
Is gibbous over Lesbos' forgone pities.
Till then cicada claps and livid beetle-runners
Scour Pompeii's courtesans and cindery tanners.

With burning eyes the Centaurs gather,
Plume tails and wink, and cover mouths and whisper
Of Thracian girls, then smirk and groom their hair.

The Sun, a slowing yellow Flange,
Mellows palazzo, grange;
The goatherd ducks from bat's sway flight;
Shed lizard's tail curls up with sacred tinge;,
The whole Mediterranean stalls in evening light,
Ox-skulls on plains shine out like large and costly spanners
And rags on twigs take on the glow of holy banners:

The Centaurs are moved, yet deeper in grove
Limber their limbs, their eyes grow hot for love
Like fire in a tomb or blood in a cave.

The Sun, fat Vat labouring fast,
Bubbles red juice at the last,
Dapples with blood the Centaurs' glade.
Then packing they burst from boughs with yell and blast —
Sacking the village they clutch their girls in the raid:
Returning to wood they gutturally rape and savage them hard
Until they're dead or quiet: half-stripped, blood striped and barred.

Then panting and sweating the Centaurs by ford
Sleep out their surfeit, and slowly waken up sad
To a sun that seems a piece of round and yellow board.

For Winter comes and death to Centaur brave —
Then Skull beside a Horse-rib cage no proof
Of blood in tomb or fire in cave.

III

Autumn's Oblation

Farewell to Tangier coasts!
    return to autumn borders.
Foresaking banner suns!
       succumb to Hunter moons
Which redly copper murderesses, swarthy barrows —
Hump wombs, tree-ringed, and dumb above the damson boughs.
Pale suns, mad King, black swans and cobra lust are sighing
And over humming weirs the river runs to death.
   The river runs to the salt salt seas:
   Hanging low are the tall sad trees:
   Death is end of long wrong stream —
   O, my darling, dream.

The Priest, who's King, iron-crowned with totem, sways for
     breath;
Across autumnal river wade the brown-horsed forders.
The red-lipped leaves now part in tatter-wind with tunes;
The worm in mould-filled horn now moistly threads and burrows;
The rain-cloud shadows maunder (heavy, rusted dhows);
Wails back the upland grave the caw of heron flying.
    The heron goes to the wide white graves;
    Shining white are the cold old graves;
    Death is end of world's wide sea —
    Kiss, O darling, me.

The taloned Leader-Man dismounts for branch-gap spying,
Observes the vast old King go clambering up the heath,
(Billows his chasuble, brown-stained from altar murders
When pointed wand incised on victim liquid runes).
The corn is garnered; emptied are the varnish marrows
From all long bones and horns; and wind round Menhir blows.
    The raindrops fall on the low gray meres;
    Falling now are the sky's gray tears:
    Death at end of wide tide's reach —
    Wide the raving beach.

The gray-haired King shakes hands with oaks with mops and
   mows;
The beaked and steeple-hatted horsemen still are eyeing
The moon-lit shade of King, which flounders like a grief
Wandering through bars before the gaze of lean-lipped warders:
Elk's antlers bracket moon, which casts down glazing swoons
On basins, scaffolds, moats, and slavers idle harrows.
   The wizen leaves from the brown grown woods
   Leaving elms as gaunt worn hoods;
   Fall the woods to death's gray mounds
      Where the ocean sounds.

The circuit malice of the horsemen Killers narrows
Converging on the King like knived and beckoning prows,
With outstretched clumsy arms the purple King is crying —
With his own royal robes they swaddle him to death.
Then throbs his flesh beneath the hand and club marauders
And, as the drowning Elk in puckered marsh, he moans.
   Melt under earth the long bronze horns:
   Stuffed with ash the tired iron urns:
   Death divides your rare dear flesh —
      Kiss and keep me, kiss.

The river hums to death among the bearded dunes,
And, steaming as unladen Rood, the dead King's sorrows
Shall whiten deadly Nightshade, redden rambler snows,
Devolve on galleons. nooses, spars, high forests dying,
On pyres, on chortling boars, on all within skin's sheath,
On crumbling horns, on clanging tombs, on sour-bone girders.
   The river falls to the sore raw shore
   Rending us with the grave wave's roar:
   Death is end of love's heart smart —
      Part — my darling — part.

The King is dead on borders; under tarnished moons
The horsemen beaked are spying; with crooked mops and mows
The river hums from narrows to the bearded dunes
   With death at end of long wrong stream —
      O, my darling, dream.

IV

From Winter's World

Wrinkles earth, stiffen trees;
Vacant is the starving wold;
Idle are transparent seas
Motionless on shingles cold;
Wires of pylons faintly call
Lapsed upon the frozen mould;

For crinkled is the horn's chill lip,
From cliffs melts down on winter's dip.

Gallows creak; cusps of heath
Rasp within the twirler wind;
Pirouetting in their death
Felons shed their spotted rind:
Bearded darnels hold their guard —
Sentinels where Centaurs sinned

And scrawled with hooves their lust's gruff game.
Unhasped is now the Virgin's name.

Charred the walls, grubbing pry
Burnt indicting finger-beams
Etching smoke in tawdry sky.
Eclipsed is sun, its tiny gleams
Straggle from its blackened plate
Fidgeting from fretting rims.

But reared the Child from Virgin womb
Till hubs of pain his bones become.

Grates the ice; Centaur's skull
Fumbles in the fetid tarn;
Moats with viscous tears are full;
Tumbled is the jaded cairn;
Leaning is the citadel;
The God sweats blood from olive glen;

His Mother knows when flesh is crushed
That then is slaked his Father's thirst.

Falls the hood; cobra's dead;
Muffled is volcano's moan,
Condensed its rakish cinder load
Sealed by amber gelid zone.
The dawn is gapped by cock's red crow
Spilling tears on faithless son.

When hauled upon the splaying wood
God's robes will soak with Virgin's blood.

Blow the winds; gibbets shake
Corpses in their frailty;
Moon blisters off and flakes;
Stars retreat into the sky;
When God is flogged quaint mouths and cups
Pour stammering upon his back;

Soon glowing birds of Paradise
From Rib of Adam shall arise.

Suppurates, bisects with swirl
Sun, and coils cylindrical:
They garb the God with royal shawl,
Spike Crown of thorns imperial;
A reed of King thrust in His fist
Fulfills harped prophet's oracle:

The Cup, that by next Year's King,
With diamond dews shall spray the spring.

History ends; winter drains
The sacred wine of Son of Man,
Who's led with yells through scarlet lanes,
The dripping Hill to tread upon;
A vernicle has liquid brand:
Transfixed to bleed is Heaven's gold Sun —

He twists upon the middle Cross
And splinters all the winter's loss.

He's manned with thieves: the ladder, nail,
Iron hammer, vinegar and sponge
Wail Golgotha: the waiting Grail
Is filled from side by spear's quick lunge:
The sky swarms black: the Christ's outcries
Accuse his Father in Death's plunge.
The land is left for winter cave
With walls as red as Virgin's womb:

There lies — until, like Sun on eastern wave,
Christ rises — King, flings garlands on the tomb.

Murdock

We of this Village know our heavy Wood
Haunted by Brothers in their furious Mood.
Two Brothers, locked and pledged to nightly Duel,
Fight under Trees, hidden at fullest Moon.
Though dumb, their Blows do toss upon the Gale;
Their Groans disturb us at our Murdock Fires;
Their sobs are heard through Falls of Autumn Rain;
And Cudgel-Blows between the Thunder Roars
Come groaning out from Oak and Clumps of Beech,
With Foxgloves spattered by the Brothers' Blood —
The cursed Drops of that unhallowed Brood
That troubles Heaven and Murdock overmuch.

Each Night within the Wood they shift their Ground —
This Larch, that Elm receives another Wound.
Sometimes scuffling here, or struggling there,
Always Two Brothers dealing Monstrous Blows
Hidden from Moon, yet nightly through the Year
Bloody and straining under woeful Boughs.

We of the Village know this Pair;
And Mothers move their Children into Doors
As Nightfall comes, and comes the muttering Doom —
The Brothers battling for their fate Yard.
Yet from out the Umbrage they do never come.

The moody Brothers wage till reddening Dawn —
And Farmers say no maddened Oxen Herd
Would flatten Undergrowth so much
As truculent Brothers in their lurch
That leave on silver Beeches shining Scars.

Our Wood is huge and dark and Branches thick
Roof out the Gaze of Moon and Stars;
Its Compass large, with ample Room
For Brothers' Wars and rushing Fears
Of lonely and of an old Doom;
And Jack the Cartwright he has sworn
Each has both sullen Hoof and weird Horn.

Will the Woodsman working in the Noon
Comes back with Blood still wet upon his Boots;
He's white and shaking in the setting Sun
Because no Trees have moist and scarlet Roots,
And in the Inn we crowd around and look —
Then drink another Ale against Ill-Luck.
Last month Nell Jenkins went too close, now mad
She hears the groaning Brothers in her head.

And who are among our neighbour Villagers,
Hearing the Brothers scuffling in the Dark,
Pulls not all Blankets over Ears?
Or holds his Wife more near? Or mutters Prayers?
Or lights his Candle with a thumping Haste?
Or gropes his Way and bolts his Door more fast?
Though Reverend Evans scoffs upon our Dread
Yet he has heard and sweats upon his Bed —
For Murdock Wood is known through all the Shire.

Last Night Ted Wilks was riding Home his Mare,
And late from courting took the Murdock Road,
He reached the Gate that led into the Wood
When reared the Mare, and right up straight she stood,
She yelled her Horror from an upright Head,
With Nostrils wide and Eyes that filled up red.
Next Day she cast her Foal. It came out dead.

And Ted himself since then has kept his Bed,
Though Sexton says from Boyhood he's had Pluck.

Our Wood is huge and round and matted thick
With Boughs like Hooks that hide their Clutch;
Holes in Oaks that wink and watch;
And Weeds like Thongs that bide to catch;
Hollow Trunks that sound like Gongs;
And sudden Nightshade shoots its jets;
Monster Toadstool glistens Sweats.
Days are ill, but worse are Nights,
When cursed Brothers at their Wrongs
Wake up Murdock from its sleep,
Each of us in Terror's Grip,
And down before us is Hell's Drop,
And it is dark, and it is steep,
Hoof and Horn and Mistletoe,
Toad and Stool and Who-knows-what?
Old Nan she laughs upon her Cot
And she is bald, her Wits are fled,
And she is mad, and Who is not
Hearing Brothers from a Bed?
Nightly in the Wood they go —
Hoof and Horn and Mistletoe.

II

Ah, Murdock's Brothers are the Shire's Renown,
And Sunday Trippers drive up from the Town.
They gape and goggle, push into our Homes,
Sit down to Cakes, shake Skirts and scatter Crumbs,
Take our Photos, interfere,
Walk up and down in Coats of Fur,
Give Children Sweets and take our Cream,
Peep in the Wood and scream,
Annoy our Sexton, Nan they badger,
Mock at Dad and make a Noise,
Say Moo at Cows, throw Stones, and Hedges break,
Then climb with Streamers in a yellow Bus
Which turns the Corner in a Cloud of Smoke,
Take Care to leave before Sunset;
And leave us to our Lot.

The downing Sun is throbbing just above the Hill.
The bragging Wind gets up its usual Wail
Along the Wires and Poles. The Hill is wrapped in Mist.
Once more the evening Shadows start their bulgy Roll
In spreading Hoops on top of Murdock Wood.
Still rasps the Wind, down goes the Sun too fast,
There goes the grumpy pant of last Train out
Gathering to dimming Rattle: hear its Hoot
Before the Tunnel, meaning it has gone.
Day done; Sun down; once more in twilight now
We Folk of Murdock left to our Shire's old long Woe

With Cattle in the dank-soiled Byres,
Evans behind his studded Doors,
With Swine that trudge their plashy Sties,
The Mare behind the Stable Bars;
Old Nan upon her Hovel-floor;
The Churchyard Dead in earthen Rows;
All we of Murdock, Quick and Dead,
On wedded or on lonely Bed,
Abide the coming of the Weird

When Cows will trample down Manures,
Mare will scream and lunge behind her Bars,
And if you're wedded you will turn
To Her who shares your Bed and Bairn;
If Single then to God you'll yearn
While Animals run mad on Farm;
If Dead, you'll turn your Skeleton
To share your Terror with the Worm
Which stops to hark a Moment, till
Its gliding Entry into Skull
Make you One in such Alarm.

Who was the Mother of the Two that thump
Beneath the thundery Wood? What Woman's Womb
Bore such growing Load for nine fell Moons
And gave them Blood and Bones and her Breast Milk
To hurt this Murdock with their grisly Romp?
And has that Woman now a Graveyard-tomb
Whom these begot? And deaf to her Sons' Groans?
Or is her Dust become the Trees they knock?

Their Father who? What mankind loins
Could hoard such Brothers' Liver, Hair and Brains?
They say their Dad had Hairs enough.
His Tail was fork'd and swung with ugly luff.
He had a Snarl they say, and some, a Tusk,
A kind of sullen Hoof and weird Horn.
He to this Woman came and did his Task.
She gave them Room and bred them Blood and Bone,

Soon gave them Breasts and made them feed, while Moon
Shone full in Murdock Wood in some time long agone.

Ah, cursed are they that nightly shift their Ground!
And cursed each standing Oak their Strokes do wound!
And cursed is that on which they spill their Blood!
The Toadstool cursed whose stinks do puff and swell
With all the Sweats that from their Bodies swill!
And cursed the Brood that's done what no Man should!
The Brothers' Sin is older than the Flood
And one that Noah had shut out from his Ark;
A Sin whose Name no one has heard,
Which Holes in Oaks have only watched,
With which we're All in Murdock touched and patched. —
And now They're at it in the Dark
One Two
Mistletoe
Now they go
And Jack he hears it from his Shed,
Daft Nell she hears them round her Head,
Parson sweats and tears upon his Bed,
Old Nan she heaves and laughs upon her Cot.

Near yet nearer, now they go
Dingle Dangle Mistletoe
Toad and Tusk and Who-knows-What
Hoof and Horn and winking Hole
Swinging Tail and sudden Stool
Scarlet Root and sodden Boot
Come the Brothers at their Woe
Near yet nearer, now they go
Dingle Dangle Mistletoe.

At length the Sun gets up about its work.

We meet upon the Road outside the Inn and talk.
Jack the Cartwright says They stopped outside his Doors,
Whereon young Bert puts it, and contradicts, he says
"You think They've got a Special Grudge 'gainst You and Yours,
In point of fact, it was the other End They came,
But it's always You and Sexton wants the fame,
Although you're just the two that never takes no blame."

Then Mrs Gurton says she only heard them once before
So near, and "Mr Gurton, he will say the same,
He'll bear me out. I want no praise," she said,
"But Truth is Truth, and right outside my store they were.
I heard them clear when we had gone upstairs to Bed,
And Mr Gurton said . . ." Whereon the Sexton says,
Cuts in and says, "Of course, you never do your best
To tell us Lies, but once you said the Wind was West,
Last Monday 'twas, and then the Wind was proven East,
No, Mrs Gurton, no, I'm not the one for rows . . ."
He cough'd, look'd round, and mov'd his 'specs upon his Nose,
And says, "I heard them well. They fought outside *my* House.
But here's the Parson coming down the Road. Oh, Sir,
You know the Truth and know outside my House they were."
But Mr Evans says, although he's pale with Fear,
"Now, Good People, move along about your work,
For shame to let me find you full of Gossip-Talk.
The Brothers! Pooh! There's no such Thing!" And off he goes.
But up pipes Bert, "If that's as much our Reverend knows
Why did he 'phone the London bigwigs for a Change?

'My Lord, Murdock I cannot stand,' he said. 'It's strange',
He did I swear; I listened through a little chink,
Postmistress Mrs Stubbs she saw, she gave me a wink."
"Well, you're a saucy one," then Mrs Gurton says,
"But I've got work if Sexton's not. Good day."
Then Farmer Bunter goes to tend his Hay.
And we disperse and go about our Ways.
And set about the Fields while morning Sun
Moves big and bold till Noon, and then goes down.
And we move back to Murdock, dull and slow,
And bide once more for our Shire's Old Woe.

III
In Wet or Fine goes by each Murdock Year,
The Moody Brothers still are Murdock's Fear,
We of the village know in the Wood they are
For every Night the Pair do go about:
We dread They will, and yet They come not out.

The heavy Months are hard and drear:
We toil the Day, at Evening shake.
When Shadows lengthen, pale we look
And call to mind our deep Ill-luck,
The Blood that comes from Scarlet-Root
And ran upon the Woodman's Foot;
How he was white in setting Sun
With sullen Hoof and weird Horn.
The Year goes on, still works the Worm,
In Socket glides this clever One
While Animals run mad on Farm,
But Years go by and that we learn.
In Wet, Fine, Summer, Winter Toil
Our old Ones die, the young Ones court;
Daft Nell sways by and Life is short.
In Wood the Oak has watching Hole,
They come not out and still they brawl.

Goes by the year, in Wet or Fine,
And Washing's taken from the Line,
Round sways the Wind and swings the Vane,
The Hill's in Mist and falls the Rain.
And Mrs Stubbs runs down the Lane,
And beats her Door to let her in,
And all are patched with Brothers' Sin,
Our Chimneys roar and Rain runs down the Pane,
The Darkness creeps, the Brothers go about,
We dread They will, and yet They come not out.

Years pass, Dawns break, Dusk comes again.
Old Nan has Cancer bad and screams with Pain;
Young Tom and Jane lie down in roadside Ditch —
Her Bastard Child will get the Murdock Patch.
The Months go by, our Sexton dies, Winds roar,
The Brothers battle in the fallen Snow.
Old Nan lies dead and bald within her Hut.
We dread They will, and yet They come not out.

Round swings the Vane, and gleams its Weathercock,
Adrift in Spray, yet glistening in the Shock
Of dancing April Shine on Spire and Shack.
Young Bert's grown-up, becomes a swagger Rake
Until he hears the Brothers tussle in the Dark —
Our Bert so spry then on his Bed does shake.
He hears the Thud and knows They go about,
He fears They will, and They come not out.

Still turns the Vane, and August comes out hot.
Ted Wilks has got his Girl, his Mare is dead.
We drink fresh Ale and work in noontide blaze
And creaking Waggons end our Harvest Days.
At end of Days begins the heavy Night
And married Ones will hold their Mates more tight —
We dread They will, and yet They come not out.

Turns the Weathervane, once more fall Rains,
And Nell goes shambling down the muddy Lanes,
Always the Brothers moan inside her Head.
She leaves her sloven Shoe inside a Rut,
Goes limping past the Inn in Idiot state.
We drink another Ale against Ill-luck,
And say she went too close, is now a Slut.
Once more the Two to-night will Branches hack,
And that is bad but worse if They come out.

For Murdock Wood is thick and old;
The Oaks that watch are bossed and gnarled;
The Ash's Bark is soft and cold;
The Toad squats throbbing; Dock-Leaf's curled;
The running Spider gains a Leaf
Which rolls it up and keeps it furled,
Which coils it up and keeps it safe:
The Live are Dead, the Dead Alive.

The Fame of Murdock's Brothers gone afar.
The Townsfolk send us Parcels for our Fear.
Comforts they think will keep the Brothers dumb,
And Mittens keep a Murdock Child from Harm.
And they forget the Mare and Scarlet Root,
And Will's white Face and sodden Boot,
Old Nan now dead who laughed upon her Cot
(Now in her Grave she dreads They will come out).
No waxing nor no waning Moon
Has looked thorugh Boughs at weird Horn.
We of this Shire are bred and born.
We have to face these Things alone,
(What woman gave Them Blood and Bone?)
And Them we dread when every Day is done.
Though Mr Evans' left the Place and run
The Animals go mad each Night on Farm.
Though Sexton's dead, and Bert's grown-up
And One has Wife, the Other Worm,
Yet Murdock's Brothers still alarm
Lest within the Wood They do not stop —

Though sometime Mother gave Them Pap —
Lest They from out the Wood do leap.

And thus our Woe
Pale Mistletoe.

IV

You Men of Murdock do not fear!
The Two within the Wood can not come out.
But, though you dread to see and know the Pair,
It will be best to find out what They are.
The Two were there Years past — and further past —
Before whom Men of old have stood aghast.
Their Blows were heard long Time before the Flood,
Since then They've never left their heavy Wood.

And, though all Murdock dreads their Coming-out,
To know the Worst is still a sharp Delight —
There's mastery in that, but none in Doubt.

Suppose, one Night, to end our Murdock Curse,
Sudden, from Wood They swing on Border Grass
In lunging Crash, and strive each fresh-trod Yard —
(Further from Murdock marches ancient Weird)
In gnashing Tussle, Cudgel-handed,
Foam from Fangs and Bodies branded.
In this supposed Release They striding pace.
Over charging Seas, New Lands, They fling.
Untried Peasants hear Them, cowering,
Their Bodies growing vaster as They swing,
Their Shadows move like clouds across the Plain.
Bavarian Tillers, bending to their Grain,
Drop quick their Flails and run to Walls to hide
As stalking Shadows over Valleys glide.
The Brothers — struggling — reach the midmost Hills,
Stumble up the haggard Fells.
Backwards, forwards, up the Slopes They push,
Tossing through Mountain Shrubs the Brothers crash.

One flies, then sudden turns with sickening Pant
And hurls a Boulder in the bloody Hunt. —
Shrubs torn from Root; first One pursues, then flies,
At crashing upward They increase in Size.
Clenched, turning, choking, reaching higher Ground,
They gasp and moan, hurl Blows, turn snarling round
For dolorous Blows and straining Sighs,
Reach icy Peaks, are cast on background Skies. —
And there the Brothers stand, while Ocean Tides —
Heaving — gird up round the Mountain's sides.
The Two tall Shapes beneath the Alpine moon —
Their Blades now still this Hour before the Dawn.
Their lofty Tramplings on the frozen Ridges
Still; laid by their Feud and olden Grudges.
The Fighting still. In Snow They Stand like Flame,
Haughty yet calm, and their quiescent Eyes —
Like Martyrs' — shine from mastered Mysteries.
In quick White Marvelling of the frozen Moon
They stand, — not only heard, but, radiant, known.
Then, leaning back Their Heads, in shining Tears
Suddenly They sing upon the scattered Stars
A Sudden Song that suddenly loosens Fears —
All fears, from bleeding Womb to bloodied Hearse,
Endured by Man or by the Universe.
These to the Song streamed down in Spears
Whose raining Arcs slipped into Sea, which shook
With bars of Foam dissolving all it took.
And still They sing, in Snow They sing like Flame —
For Murdock's Brothers are the World's new Fame,
Its high, unborn and glistering Renown,
Its present Dread resplendent in its future Crown.